AFRICA ON A DARE

A Hunting Trip to South Africa at Age 70

by

Martin D. Conyac

To Lorrie,

for her love, support, and encouragement

SOUTH AFRICA
National capital
Provincial capital
Town, village
Major airport
International boundary
Provincial boundary
Main road
Railroad
ZIMBABWE
Save
Musina (Messina)
MOZAMBIQUE
NORTHERN PROVINCE
Limpopo
BOTSWANA
Polokwane (Pietersburg)
Gaborone
Nelspruit
Xai-Xai
Barberton
Delagoa Bay
NAMIBIA
Mafikeng
Johannesburg
Pretoria
Witbank
Maputo
Lüderitz
Keetmanshoop
Krugersdorp
Germiston
GAUTENG
MPUMALANGA
Mbabane
NORTH WEST
Klerksdorp
Vereeniging
Piet Retief
SWAZILAND
Hotazel
Orkney
Volksrust
Madadoni
Mkuze
Sishen
Welkom
Kroonstad
Newcastle
Vryheid
Karasburg
Bohlokong
Ulundi
Upington
Kimberley
FREE STATE
Bethlehem
Ladysmith
River View
Oranjemund
Alesander Bay
Richards Bay
Port Nolloth
Kenhardt
Bloemfontein
Maseru
K W A Z U L U - N A T A L
Stanger
Nababeep
Springbok
LESOTHO
Pietermaritzburg
Durban
Amanzimtoti
NORTHERN CAPE
Carnarvon
De Aar
Aliwal North
Drakensberg Range
Port Shepstone
Bitterfontein
Williston
Middelburg
Umtata
Port St Johns
Calvinia
Victoria West
Queenstown
Klawer
EASTERN CAPE
Beaufort West
Graaff-Reinet
Bisho
Saint Helena Bay
Vredenburg
Saldanha
WESTERN CAPE
Oudtshoorn
Grahamstown
East London
Paarl
Worcester
George
Uitenhage
Port Alfred
Cape Town
Stellenbosch
Heidelberg
Knysna
Port Elizabeth
Strand
Cape of Good Hope
Cape St. Francis
Table Bay
Cape Agulhas
Mossel bay
Algoa Bay
SOUTH ATLANTIC OCEAN
INDIAN OCEAN
Capital:
Pretoria, administrative;
Cape Town, legislative and
Bloemfontein, judicial
0 100 200 300 km
0 100 200 mi
SOUTH AFRICA
Marion I. (S.A.)
The boundaries and names shown and the designations used on this map do not imply official endorsement or acceptance by the United Nations.

CONTENTS

Introduction

As I get older I find myself seeking out the pleasures of this life that have evaded me for 70 years. Most people call this process their to-do list or "bucket list" and it usually consists of activities such as foreign travel, safaris, skydiving, entertainment, climbing some mountain, owning a Bentley, gourmet food and drink, and having or doing anything else different and exciting, and within grasp according to physical and financial limitations.

But as the items on the bucket list get completed and lined out, are there other things that surface to replace them? Is it God's will that Man is always wanting? Unfortunately, yes. There is simply no end to 'wants', no matter how young or old, rich or poor, etc. The bucket list is endless. In my humble opinion, when it comes to bucket lists, a hunting trip to wild, natural South Africa should be on it for everyone— man, woman, or child—and no one ever realizes it until after they've done it. My wife Lorrie and I did it and didn't even know it was on the list.

Throughout the narrative of this writing I use the term "safari" loosely— very loosely. Reading about the history of the safaris as they were, when embarked upon in the mid-1800's by the first European explorers of South Africa, will make it apparent that this was merely an escorted hunting trip, not a safari.

This is said not to discount the fun and great value of this once-in-a-lifetime adventure, but only to put it in perspective with the scope and deeper purpose of the original safaris.

The following brief background information is gleaned from the wonderful, illustrated 383-page book by Bartle Bull, "*Safari—A Chronicle of Adventure*" published by Carroll & Graf 2006:

"Missionaries, prospectors, explorers, and ivory hunters were the first travelers to Africa's interior lands, but they killed animals mostly for food to sustain their other interests, and their focus was not on the sporting pursuit of the abundant game as is a true safari. What came to be called a safari was a sustained sporting expedition in the African bush that took months or years of planning, long sailing voyages from England with shiploads of wagons and equipment, and spanned several years or even a decade. Financed mainly by the ivory taken from the largest animals, and skins and meat of others, these early "sportsmen" were given passage through the land by supplying the local villagers with meat and ivory from the large and dangerous game that would otherwise be difficult to get by the natives by use of their primitive weapons.

"Those early safaris were journeys of exploration, discovery, science, and documentation of the then unknown flora and fauna of the interior of the Dark Continent. There were no laws or limits on the white hunters and they fairly went where they wanted and killed as much as they wanted when they wanted. Explorers such as botanist William Burchell who in 1810 sailed to Cape Town, took six months just to plan his trip into the interior to study and collect plants and to attempt to penetrate deeper into the interior than any white man before. He commissioned the design and construction of a sturdy wagon to haul all the gear and equipment to sustain an extended journey, and that "Cape" wagon eventually found its way to the American West later in the 19th century. Burchell ate 23 species of antelope and "discovered" (named) several including the sassaby, brindled gnu (blue wildebeest), and of course the Burchell zebra. He lived off the land and was totally self-sufficient, and his home was wherever he happened to be. His journey was for botany, not hunting, but its elements would inspire and share much with the first true safaris that came 25 years later.

"Some believe it was Sir William Cornwallis Harris that would establish the tradition of the great African safaris. He studied the drawings of Burchell and read of his adventurous accounts, and at a young age was determined to someday commit to a prolonged hunting safari into the uncolonized interior of what is now South Africa. In 1836 he embarked on a two-year journey—to slaughter the proud giraffe— and to "discover something new." Being first displayed to Julius Caesar in Rome the giraffe wasn't something new, but was considered the ultimate tribute or gift to someone who already had everything. Different hunters had different favorites, and to Harris, a student of wildlife mythology, the giraffe, or camelopard, represented the magic of African wildlife. Among other things, his gear included two Cape wagons, 42 oxen, 12 horses, and of course many men, food, liquor, coffee, tools, guns, powder, and 18,000 prepared bullets and raw lead and moulds to make more bullets. (For comparison, I only spent 20 rounds of the 60 total that I took to Africa for this one-week hunt.) Also a naturalist and obsessed with accuracy, Harris would meticulously document the animals he killed by repeatedly measuring them and carefully drawing them in proportion. The oryx excited him and he agreed with others that this antelope was probably the source of the legend of the unicorn, which was traceable back to ancient Egypt and Persia. The oryx, or gemsbok, has exceptional endurance and will to live, has been known to kill lions, and when wounded is dangerous to approach. It has poker-straight horns about 3-feet long, and when viewed in profile or when one horn is broken off, it closely resembles the depictions of the fabled unicorn. It is thought that Harris might have been the first European to shoot a waterbuck, but it is reported that he was disappointed at the rank, carrion-like smell of its flesh. Cornwallis Harris was the first white man to shoot and document the regal Sable antelope, distinguished by its glossy black coat, white belly, and black and white blazed face, with long, curving scimitar horns five feet long arching back over its shoulders. For generations the 500-pound antelope was known as the Harris Buck.

"Men like Roualeyn Gordon Cumming, William Cotton Oswell, and William Charles Baldwin, mostly fiercely independent and somewhat eccentric, all left writings rich with safari adventures that included danger, gore, disease, native conflicts, and many other hardships. Cumming once chased a female oryx so long on a hot, dry day that after he shot her he sprang from his horse as she fell and drank the warm milk from her teats. In five years, Cumming lost 45 saddle horses, 70 dogs, and 70 oxen to lions, sickness, and other causes.

"In large part, the notable men of the early safaris were gentlemen of pedigree and durable physique, with distinguished educations and military, athletic, or other personal accomplishments. They were men of courage and skills, and had a passion for discovery of the unknown. Their philosophies were somewhat different, as between Cumming and Oswell. For Cumming, safaris were a visceral and passionate sport and the thrill was in the killing. It released the uncompromising urges of man as a primitive hunter and no matter how much he shot, the bag was never enough—wounds and waste were of no account. For Oswell, shooting was just a part of the overall enjoyment of an outdoor, adventurous life, to be done properly as a gentleman does everything, and with a sense of standards and fairness. As later observers have commented, it is difficult to conceal one's character on safari, even from one's self.

"Determined to hunt elephants, Frederick Courtenay Selous would become the greatest of all the white hunters. By 1870 elephants were virtually extinct in the Transvaal, and even resourceful ivory hunters found it difficult to make a living in South Africa. Selous arrived in South Africa in 1871 but by then the land of Cumming and Harris was changing rapidly. By 1860 buffalo, lion, elephant, and rhino were already extinct in the Orange Free State. As early as the 1850's, 30,000 elephants were killed each year in what was to become Kenya, Tanganyika, and Uganda according to some estimates. By 1880 that number was 60,000 to 70,000. Selous killed hundreds of elephants, hunted mostly on foot, and had so many close calls and exciting experiences, that his writings were noted by a young English diplomat posted in South Africa in the 1870's that became the first important African novelist. That novelist was H. Rider Haggard whose fictional hero was patterned after Selous as the great white hunter Allan Quatermain of King Solomon's Mines and other adventure novels. In 1903 Selous visited the White House and served as the inspiration for Teddy Roosevelt to begin his great safari that began in April of 1909.

"In the first safaris, tsetse flies killed horses and men. Nearly everyone contracted malaria of some degree, depending on the type of malaria and their personal biological resistance. Physical injury from accidents and encounters with wild animals was common. Slavery was rampant between the warring tribes, and in political and personal relationships slavery had to be dealt with according to one's tolerance for it or willingness to please some territorial tribal king or monarch. Passage through some territories was more hazardous from the human inhabitants than from the wild animals, disease, hardships, or environment. Rifles and firearms were muzzleloaders, not the effective, efficient, and powerful arms of today's modern hunter, and were loaded on the run either afoot or on horseback to continue shooting until an animal fell, perhaps after 20 shots. Large dangerous game was a genuine challenge to hunt with those guns, whose power was limited and whose reliability was questionable. Due to hardships the crew would often abandon the hunter, leaving him stranded and alone to fend for himself in the bush, with limited supplies and miles from nowhere.

"The visceral fulfillment of hunting explains why, even when it is not essential for food, it has been one of man's most pleasurable and sought-after activities. This is why the privileged have made it their chosen recreation, from Pharaoh Rameses II with his hunting chariot in 1270 BC, to Chairman Lenin with his powered hunting sled in 1920. In ancient Macedonia, in Victorian Bengal, and in contemporary Hungary and Tanzania, the big game has been reserved for the privileged, whether by position or by wealth. In the United States, where hunting is more democratic than it is in Europe or Africa, there are today more than 17,000,000 licensed hunters. In their later years, most of the early safari hunters seemed to regret the wanton killing of the thousands of animals that died at their hand, and they became concerned

with the conservation and preservation of the dwindling African game. They promoted some of the first movements to control and license hunters and to manage the well-being, reproduction, and management of the game, and promoted the ideas of setting aside special land for game preserves."

The slaughter of the African animals in the last half of the 1800's somewhat paralleled the slaughter of the bison on the open plains of the central and western United States. Many species were hunted to near extinction. The great African safaris lasted for roughly one century. From 1836 until 1939 unique conditions and eccentric individuals created a style of adventure that can never exist again. Abundant big game, ungoverned landscapes, suitable weapons, the lifelong habit of hunting, a zest for discovery and an appreciation of both hardship and luxury, all came together then in the vast bush of Africa. But now in modern times over most of Africa, hunting (and Professional Hunters) is either prohibited or highly regulated. All legal hunting was stopped in Kenya in 1977, and many other countries have since implemented stringent regulations, so that now many of the former professional hunters have either quit the profession, or traded in their guns for cameras.

To others, the rich and adventurous history of the original safaris is much more exciting to read than the write up of this African trip, but to me the personal experience beats reading about the experiences of others hands down.

It's interesting the turns that life takes as the years unfold one by one. As a younger person I never dreamed of some of the things that are actually happening in my 71st year of life, things that I might have thought of but never really believed would happen to me.

To begin with, in anticipation of my 70th birthday in February 2012, my wonderful wife Lorrie dedicated herself to making this year the most memorable of all my years so far. So she started the year with a big surprise birthday party for me (which really was a surprise) at the home of a good friend, where she presented me with airline tickets to Hawaii, plus tickets for an ocean cruise for a week of tripping around some of the islands and leisurely lounging in Honolulu. It was fabulous as it fulfilled two items on my "bucket list" of, first, taking a real cruise on a luxury ship, and second, of visiting the only remaining state in the USA that I had never visited.

In April, Lorrie booked us for several days at a penthouse suite at a resort overlooking Lake Coeur d' Alene, Idaho, where we shared the weekend with some good friends from Spokane. Then in May at a fundraiser dinner for the Friends of the National Rifle Association, she encouraged me to bid in an auction for a seven-day hunting safari in South Africa. Little did I know that this event would be a huge Y in the road that we would take on our road through life.

The seven-day hunt was advertised as a $5,000 to $6,000 value, complete with $2,000 towards the fee for the animals that we would shoot, plus $1,000 towards the taxidermy cost of mounting the trophies that we would collect. As in any auction, the bids started out low, so with Lorrie's encouragement I bid by holding up my bright yellow card when the auctioneer called for a bid of a few hundred dollars. I continued to bid as the bid climbed to near a thousand dollars, and then by about $1,250 nearly everyone bidding had dropped out. As this was a five- to six-thousand-dollar item, the price still seemed like a bargain, so again at Lorrie's urging I continued to bid until the bid reached $1,650 at which point the hunt was given to me and one other competitive bidder. So we won an honest-to-God African shooting safari worth $6,000 for the bargain sum of $1,650! Now this was something totally "outside the box" from anything we had ever done or even dreamed of doing in our entire life, and we were excited about the prospect of the exotic adventure in a far-away land. In the back of our minds we knew that this cost would only be the start of something rather expensive for us, but we took the mindset that if we were going to do it, we'd go all out and do it to the best of our ability within the limitations of our budget. We won the hunting trip at the auction in early May and it allowed us to schedule the safari for anytime from then until the end of 2013. Lorrie suggested that we schedule the trip for the summer of 2013, but at our age and with the uncertainty of the economy and the situation of world politics, I suggested that sooner would be better than later. Who knows what things would be like in 2013. So we scheduled the seven-day hunt such that we would leave home in Blaine, Washington, September 30, put feet on the ground in Johannesburg October 1, and be back home October 10, 2012.

With our great anticipation of the trip, the summer (now in retrospect) seemed to fly by. By the time we bought wardrobes of boots and real safari clothes, a new scope for the Winchester Model 70 .308 caliber rifle (that I've owned for 47 years), and paid for loads of practice ammo, several doctor visits for immunizations to a host of foreign diseases, and of course the airline tickets round-trip for two to South Africa, plus other extra fees and expenses for the safari (including lots of tips), plus the cost of shooting a couple more animals than we originally planned, plus the all-important physical proof of the success of our trip, the trophies with full taxidermy treatment, and souvenirs from the local bazaar, we figured that the total expense would settle at just about $22,000. So much for the safari at a bargain price of $1,650. Hey, if you want to play you have to pay! After talking to other people that have hunted in South Africa, I (and they) still believe we got this once-in-a-lifetime experience at a bargain price.

But we knew that at our age, and because of the long uncomfortable flight, and the expense, this would be the only time in our life that we'd do it, so we took on the challenge of going on this real African safari.

On the South African Airlines plane, seated 8 across on the Airbus A320.

Lorrie, bless her energetic and generous little heart, made all the arrangements with the Numzaan Safaris Company, all the flight reservations on South African Airlines, and the shuttle reservations to and from the Seattle airport. My work consisted of the planning and preparation of the equipment, practicing shooting at the gun range, making doctor appointments, and finalization of the mounds of paperwork to get our rifle in and out of the USA and in and out of South Africa. Fortunately, John Campbell, the safari representative that sold us the trip at the auction, was a big help in starting the paperwork, and we paid a representative in Johannesburg $100 to finalize our paperwork for the South African Police Service (SAPS) to assure our seamless transition in and out of the country with our rifle. The complex eight-page SAPS form had to be filled out perfectly, and the $100 we spent for the representative that met us at the airport was well worth the expense. We breezed right through the police and customs both going there and coming home, although there were some anxious moments when we had to search for misplaced papers to satisfy the needs of the police and customs.

Professional Hunter Jean-Louis Viljoen in the back of the Mahindra truck, made in India.

The trip to South Africa began with a three-hour ride on the airport shuttle from Bellingham to Seattle, where we stayed overnight. Early the next morning we took a five-hour nonstop flight from Seattle to the Dulles Airport at Washington, D.C. where we changed planes and waited for an hour and a half. We then flew seven hours nonstop from Dulles to Dakar, Senegal, where we landed for fuel and some passengers but weren't allowed to deplane. A couple hours later we continued the seven-hour nonstop flight from Dakar to Johannesburg. Lorrie had the good foresight to buy us some compression socks for our legs, and they actually made the trip much more comfortable. We wore them the entire time while traveling to and from South Africa. It was a relief to finally get off the airplane in spite of having a relatively good flight, but the trip still wouldn't be over until we drove an additional three hours to get to our hunting lodge about 150 miles north-northwest of Johannesburg. We were met at the Johannesburg airport by our Professional Hunter (PH), Jean-Louie Viljoen, who would take responsibility for us until he delivered us back to the airport eight days later. It was a long day by the time we fell into bed at the Kamboo Lodge, about 120 miles west of Polokwane, near the Limpopo river. Although the next morning would be our first official day of hunting, we didn't get up until we felt rested, which was after only about seven hours of sleeping. Surprisingly, the long, 10,750-mile flight and 9-hour time zone change wasn't as hard to adjust to as I

Back of the Kamboo Lodge, with PH Jean-Louis standing by the fire pit. The lawn and trees were green because of the irrigation.

thought it would be and we were eagerly up at five a.m. each of the following mornings to begin the hunt at six. But coming home was painful; it took an entire week to readjust to the ten-hour time zone change and readjust our bio-rhythms, probably because we both came down with a cold about half way through the week while hunting.

Life at the Kamboo lodge was easy and relaxed. The food was great and although breakfast at 5:30 was usually fruit, coffee, juice, cold meat, cheese and cereal, each lunch and dinner had wild game served in a variety of ways along with good side dishes and salads, pasta, fabulous desserts, and ample beverages of your choice. Our bed was a bit firm for my liking, but the rooms were nicely furnished, clean, well-lighted, and had real toilets and showers with plenty of hot water. I believe the water was pure and drinkable, but since plenty of bottled water was furnished we took advantage of it and drank gallons of it over the course of the week. With daytime temperatures over 100 degrees we needed to stay well hydrated. Outside the rear of the main lodge was a large paved area with lawn chairs surrounding a round, eight-foot-diameter concrete fire pit that was always burning with a wood fire to welcome us to dinner each evening. The dining area was exclusively for us as we were the only hunting clients this first week of October, which was essentially the end of the hunting season. Our laundry was done daily, the room was

Outside the fence at the front of the Kamboo Lodge. Note the jacaranda tree in bloom at right.

made up twice daily, and we got real special treatment at every meal. The grounds were tastefully landscaped with native and non-native trees, cactus, and a generous, irrigated lawn area, with a surrounding fence to keep the wild animals out. Often we would see nyala and kudu browsing near the fence. In the front of the lodge was a huge jacaranda tree in full bloom with its beautiful large, medium-blue trumpet-shaped flowers. The jacaranda stood out from the dark, bare surrounding trees, still naked in their winter habitat, and it was visible for miles when our location in the bush was just right. This was far from camping like I did for years as a field geologist when I slept in tents in a sleeping bag and ate many cold meals from a tin can. This was my kind of safari! The Kamboo Lodge was one of about five lodges used for hunters by the Numzaan Safari Company. The lodges were scattered around the Limpopo Province at locations favorable for the particular game that was to be hunted. Obviously, each game animal preferred a particular habitat and thus the lodges were in those habitats.

The Kamboo Lodge was the home and ranch house (including many out-buildings) of a former cattle

Tagged Cape Buffalo waiting for end of quarantine before being turned loose. Although they were fenced, we didn't mess with these bad boys.

ranch, and the property consisted of about 7,000 acres of bush, grass plains, and a sliver of lush, green jungle along the Crocodile River. Cattle ranching was no longer practiced, the property instead having reverted to nature and the domain of the local native wild animals. Some animals had been imported to the ranch over the years and allowed to breed, and others such as Cape Buffalo were brought in specifically for quarantine before being turned loose to run wild. Near the lodge were some sturdy fenced areas containing over a dozen huge, ear-tagged Cape Buffalo, some rare Sable antelope, exotic nyala antelope with their lyre-shaped horns, and a herd of about 30 eland, the largest of the antelopes (about 1500 pounds) with spiral horns and light beige skins. In the bush we encountered giraffe, waterbuck, zebra,

An exotic nyala antelope, all $3,125 worth, required a 10-day booking to hunt.

wildebeest, hartebeest, gemsbok, blesbok, steenbok, duiker, jackals, monkeys, baboons, ostrich, and plenty of the constantly

running Southern Impala and warthogs. The beautiful gray kudu with their pretty delicate faces, large round ears, and magnificent spiral horns were everywhere, and being tall, the kudu seemed to serve as the lookout for danger for the other animals. Our PH saw tracks of a leopard near a water hole one morning, but we never saw any large cats or other dangerous game. Elephants, lions, rhino, and hippos weren't known to be in this area. The native birds were beautiful, varied, and entertaining, especially when we'd watch them while we sat silent for hours in the blinds at the watering holes. Flocks of guinea fowl were plentiful. Only one snake was pointed out --to Lorrie-- on this trip, and we saw a spider the size of a small dessert plate in the lodge one evening, but nobody smashed it (like I would have) because they said it kept down the other bugs! The most unusual animal we saw looked like a small rabbit but it ran by jumping with its back legs just like a little kangaroo. As for the plants in the bush, only a few were without stickers or thorns and I believe I never had the good luck to encounter any of them. The fishhook thorns of everything else would tie me up soundly and snatch the hat from my head if I got careless or in a hurry to stalk an animal being pursued by our PH. You didn't just push your way through this brush. We were in South Africa just at the end of its dry winter season, and the week was blessed with clear blue skies and dry warm weather until it began getting overcast on the last day of our hunt. Rain in Johannesburg was reported on the day we drove to the airport, and by then you could see a faint green blush coming over the bush all across the dry, brown landscape. Spring was bursting forth and the rainy season was just beginning when we left.

Our driver, tracker, and skinner Andries, with Lorrie, and with Vuvu, the PH's female Jack Russell terrier.

On the first morning of our hunt our PH introduced us to his assistant, a young black man named Andries who would serve as our driver while the PH stood on the truck tailgate spotting animals. Andries was also an excellent spotter and tracker, and would skin the game we took and prepare the hides and heads for later handling by the taxidermist. He was quiet and mild mannered, and his slow steady gait was unwavering and somewhat mesmerizing, as he seemed to never get excited or hurried. He had two speeds— slow and stop.

Lorrie on day one. We dressed for the cool mornings of temps in the high 50's.

He seemed pleasant but his English was very limited so we hardly spoke with him, and all his direction came from the PH in Afrikaans, the form of Dutch language brought to the Cape by Protestant settlers in the 17th century. It seemed that everyone we encountered was multi-multi-lingual, as South Africa has about a dozen "official" languages including English, Xhosa, Zulu, Afrikaans, and several others.

The first day of the hunt was relaxed as we were still recovering from the long flight and the ten-hour time zone change, so we didn't show up for breakfast until about 7:30. We weren't on the truck hunting until after 8:00 and most of the morning was spent driving some of the roads and getting us used to the routine. Our PH took Lorrie on a couple of stalks of impala and blesbok, but with so many pairs of eyes keeping track of them, it was hard to get close enough for a good shot. We came in for brunch at about noon, and as the established daily routine we didn't go back out to hunt until the heat of the day began wearing off at about three o'clock. We would then hunt until after sunset by driving the roads through the bush or by setting in a blind established at one of the several watering holes. There were natural ponds that the animals came to for water, but there were also some concrete water containers left over from the days of cattle ranching that had

Checking the zero on the scope and rifle after the flight and before starting the hunt.

water pumped to them to keep them supplied with water. The winter "dry season" would evaporate all the water quickly if it weren't resupplied by the water wells that were reportedly as deep as 900 feet. Most of the ranch acreage was fenced, some by low fences and some by fencing

Serious stalk—the sticks are set and the scope dust covers are up!

eight to ten feet high that was reinforced so that it would contain any animals that didn't have the ability to dig under it. Even the agile, bounding impala that could leap 20 or 30 feet in distance could only jump fencing as high as five or six feet. Interestingly, some of the animals we saw crossing fences didn't jump the fences but went under them. We witnessed a herd of about 20 or more gemsbok running full speed under a short fence, and wondered why they didn't just jump it. When they hit the fence at full speed their long straight horns seemed to lift the fence like a wedge as they shot their noses under the bottom and kept moving at full speed. It was a spectacular event to witness, as the fencing didn't seem to slow these 550-pound animals one bit. The impala would jump a low fence along one side of the road by beginning their jump completely from the opposite side of the road. It was a beautiful spectacle to watch them jump, take an Olympian pose with their front legs tucked back, heads up, backs arched and hind legs extended, and gracefully glide the entire distance over the road and fence. It was almost like seeing them in slow motion; they looked just like the emblem on the Chevy Impala cars!

In our search for animals, many of the roads we drove were along the perimeter of the property and were fenced on one side with the high fencing, obviously intended to confine the animals. The former cattle ranch was private property, and as such, in South Africa anything on the property belonged to the land owner, wild animals included. There were no hunting seasons, no bag limits, and no hunting license needed to hunt on this private property. And no restrictions on hours of hunting, or limitations on which animals could be taken. The animals were private property and the land owner negotiated (?) with the safari company to set the price for each animal. Want to take a cape buffalo? Cough up $17,500 at this ranch. You could bag a southern roan for $13,973 or a sable for $14,329. The nyala were cheaper at $3,125 and you could even hunt leopards for $3,500. One of the most desirable trophy animals was the beautiful spiral-horned kudu that was priced at $4,882 if you got one with horns greater than 55 inches. These prices pretty well explain why we chose to shoot a common blesbok ($551), blue wildebeest ($1,379), gemsbok ($1,653), southern impala ($495), red hartebeest ($1,552), and a warthog

The regal Sable antelope.

($447). But price wasn't the only restriction, as the safari company required that you book at least ten days in order to hunt certain animals, depending on their rarity or difficulty to hunt, or for instance whether or not they were to be hunted at night. Another restriction for us was the wall space for trophies at our house!

By the second day we were fairly rested and acclimated to the time zone change, the warm dry weather, and the routine of driving and stalking to find game. We were up at 4:45 and on the truck by six o'clock. We saw our first giraffe, standing impressively posed near the road as we rounded a corner in the truck. During the course of the day I got to stalk a blesbok and a gemsbok, but both spooked and ran. As we drove around, we also spotted two old, red hartebeest bulls that the PH passed up, and later this would be remembered as a mistake on our part, as when we wanted to find a hartebeest later, we couldn't, and didn't find ANY until the last hour of the last day of hunting, way beyond sunset when it was totally dark. Lunch was our first introduction to gemsbok jerky, and gemsbok sausage which was dry, crumbly, and dark, but very tasty.

On day two, Jean-Louis and Andries check the motion sensitive camera at a waterhole. Leopard tracks and blood were nearby.

Most of the action on the second day was for Lorrie. It seemed that all day was spent with her following the PH in pursuit of herds of Southern Impala and blesbok. With so many eyes looking for danger, the herd animals were hard to get close to. If one of them even twitched, the entire herd would take off running through the dense brush and thorny, scrubby trees. The best bet seemed to find an old, lone bull or ram that was beyond breeding and had been kicked out of the herd. These animals were the oldest, and therefore the ones with trophy horns, and also the best to be thinned from the stock because of the

Central room at Kamboo Lodge with two spiral horned kudu (center) flanked by waterbuck trophies over entrance door to dining room. The left table had coffee and hot chocolate, and the right table had fruit drinks, all available, day or night.

limited availability of natural food, and sometimes because of their feeble condition which made them close to their inevitable death and recycling as food for the predators. Hunting the "trophy" animals was simply good game management for the land owner, and the most satisfying experience for the paying client. Although Lorrie got a lot of exercise, neither of us shot at anything on day two, but it was still fun chasing the wildebeest, blesbok, and impala back and forth through the bush.

Central room at Kamboo Lodge, with Cape Buffalo (center) flanked by two blue wildebeest trophies over the door to the TV and lounge area. The white liquor cabinet to the left was always open, free with no limits.

Part II - The Hunt

*It is difficult to conceal one's character on safari,
even from one's self.*

On day three we were again up by five o'clock and on the truck by six. In the first two days of the seven-day hunt, we hadn't bagged any of the six animals we wanted in spite of seeing and stalking herds of blesbok, gemsbok, impala, and wildebeest several times. In my mind this was averaging badly, statistically. We started a seven day hunt for six species of game and were now looking at only five remaining days to get six. After seeing several animals on the move (no animal in Africa seems to stand still for very long—it's a recipe for death), and witnessing the impala leap the road, the PH spotted an old bull wildebeest that he wanted to stalk. He snapped his fingers and the driver came to an immediate stop. We jumped from the truck, and after assuring that my rifle was on "safe" and the scope dust covers were up, I followed Jean-Louis through the bush. He always grabbed his shooting sticks from the truck and led the way on the stalks, while I tried to shadow him as best I could, trying to make it appear that there was only one person as viewed by the animals if we were spotted. After glassing the animal with his binoculars to see if it was a young bull, a pregnant cow, or a trophy worth taking, Jean-Louis quickly planted his shooting

The wildebeest was way down through the tunnel of trees at the tip of the rifle in this photo. Camera date is a day off due to the big time zone change.

14

sticks. This was my signal to brace my rifle and get ready to take a shot. The challenge would be for me to pick out from the herd the animal that he intended for me to shoot. To me, from a hundred yards away and in the cover of dark, thorny brush, one wildebeest looked like another. Jean-Louis would say that the animal was, for example, the third one from the left, turned sideways, or walking a certain direction, and I'd have to question him or repeat to him to verify that we were both looking at the same animal. I certainly didn't want to shoot a "wrong" animal after he had gone to the trouble to identify and isolate a trophy specimen. He could tell from over 100 yards away whether or not the horns were trophy size, or whether the animal was a female, and if so, whether or not it was pregnant. He had amazing eyes, and could tell a lot about an animal if only seeing it at a glance, like when one would bolt across the roadway ahead of the truck.

So after a careful stalk on this third morning of hunting, with my rifle braced on the shooting sticks of the PH, I found myself gazing through the tube of my rifle's telescope down a tunnel of clearing through the bush at an old, blue wildebeest bull about 100 yards away that was looking straight at me as he stood behind a tangle of sticks and brush. I said something to Jean-Louis about my concern about the bullet being deflected by the brush, and he quickly retorted "take the shot!" Looking head-on at us at that distance made the chest of the animal look about an inch wide, but I carefully aimed below his chin low enough to make a good chest shot and squeezed the trigger. In the quiet of the stalk, the shot from the .308 sounded to me like a small military canon as it rang out through the bush, and Lorrie later said she heard the shot loud and clear as she sat in the truck a hundred

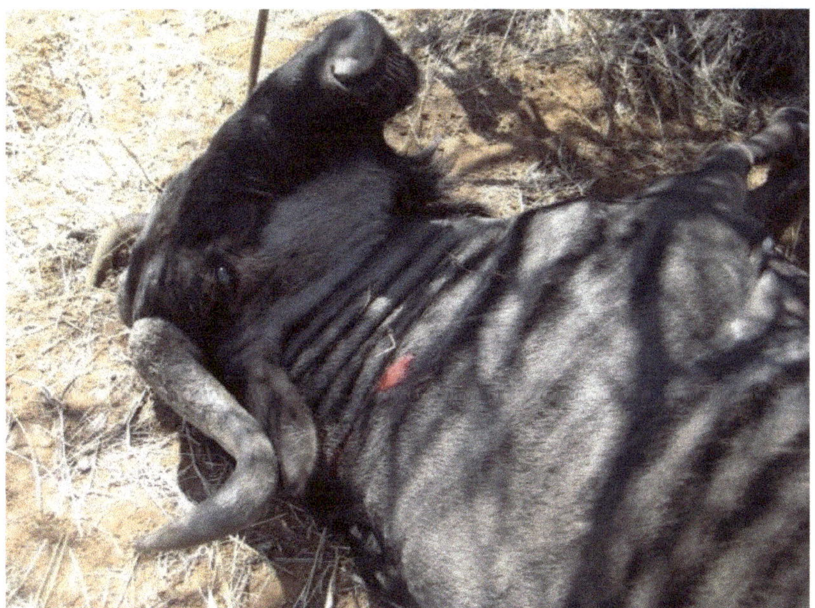

yards away wondering what was happening. The wildebeest instantly lurched to the right and dropped to the ground on his left side with his belly facing us. To me it looked like an instant kill, but Jean-Louis didn't move as his stare was frozen through his binoculars, and he cautioned me to be ready to take another shot in case it got up to run. Well, not being one to take unnecessary chances, I figured that if I could still see the body, why wait for that chance? I wanted to nail him to the ground, so I shot him again just to make sure, and he didn't budge. That second shot went low into the underbelly near the ribcage, and about a minute later when we approached the wildebeest, we saw that the first shot had broken the spine low on the neck near the body, killing the animal instantly and making the second shot totally unnecessary. On the first shot I blinked and didn't see where the bullet hit, but apparently just as I shot the bull dipped its head as it turned to run, and put his spine in the perfect position. I commented that I thought it was a really good shot, but Jean-Louis recognized it as luck, and said that he'd take luck over skill anytime! In any case, this was my first African trophy, and it was a great ego booster to down it with one shot, lucky or not. Jean-Louis extended his hand in congratulations and said "Well done Sir" which I appreciated.

No words can describe the feeling of posing with your first African big game trophy. According to the Safari Club International (SCI) scoring, this blue wildebeest bull was in the Silver category. I gnu I could get him!

    After positioning the animal for a photo session with the Great White Hunter to document the occasion, the PH and his assistant Andries muscled the animal into the back of the truck with the aid of a winch and we headed for the skinning shed. Andries quickly proceeded to do his part to assure that the animal was carefully skinned, and that the hide and horns were properly prepared in order to have a nice specimen for the taxidermist. All the identifying tags were attached to the head, hide, and horns, and since it was about noon, we went to the lodge to have brunch and lounge around until the main heat of the day was past. Coincidentally, brunch consisted of Sheppard's Pie made with wildebeest meat, accompanied by a chutney and curry noodle salad. Good stuff!

After brunch, we napped in our room for a while and at three o'clock we were on the truck again, ready for another session of hunting. So far, this day was turning out great, and now that I had gotten a trophy we had a feeling that luck was coming our way. Hours were spent each day driving the roads looking for game, or sitting for hours in blinds quietly waiting for game to frequent a nearby watering hole. This hunt was definitely not a "walk up and shoot 'em, tied-to-a-tree" type of hunt. It was fun, but it was a lot of work. We spent many hours searching for and carefully stalking each animal that we bagged, and were proud of the accomplishment.

By now on this third afternoon, Lorrie was getting pretty good at following Jean-Louis through the brush chasing game. She was still needing to shoot a blesbok or a Southern Impala to satisfy herself about the goal she had set for this hunt, and late in the afternoon when the opportunity to shoot a nice ram impala presented itself she got the rifle, braced against the shooting sticks furnished by the PH, and sighted in on his designated target animal. Lorrie was positioned right near the side of the bed of the truck. Jean-Louis had pointed out the animal, Lorrie was braced against the shooting sticks, and he was viewing the impala through his binoculars and waiting for the shot to go off. And he waited. Lorrie hesitated, and seemed to look up at him for further instructions. His bewilderment at her hesitation was palpable. Finally, I said in a loud whisper "click off the safety and shoot!" which she finally did. Earlier, Jean-Louis had told us that from the time he says to "take the shot" we generally have about three seconds. Those animals don't stand still forever, and when you find the animal in the proper position, with an acceptable view and clearance through the brush, at a reasonable distance for a successful good shot, it doesn't last for long and you need to make a quick decision to either take the shot or pass it up. And this was turning into an agonizingly long three seconds. When the silence was finally broken with the rifle's blast, the dogs came boiling out of the pickup, eager to take up a chase or a track. Lorrie and Jean-Louis started their walk up to the impala, and when they got to it they found it felled by a near perfect shot, placed back in the side and angled towards the chest as the impala was

quartering away to the right. Another second's delay and she would have missed taking what scored later as the best trophy animal of the hunt!

I believe that Lorrie herself was surprised at her success. She kept admiring the delicate beauty of the impala, and kept touching it and petting its lovely reddish brown coat. Again, as with each animal we shot, the PH posed the animal and took numerous photos of it with its horns prominently displayed and the hunter proudly smiling in the background. It was getting late in the day, so after the PH and Andries loaded the impala into the truck, we headed for the skinning shed to take proper care of the impala and to end the day with some celebration at the lodge. This third day of the hunt was one to remember, with me taking a trophy blue wildebeest in the morning, and with Lorrie taking a real winner impala in the late afternoon. The statistical success for harvesting our six designated animals on this seven-day hunt had improved.

*"Me Tarzan, you Jane." Here's Jane with the **only** SCI GOLD class trophy of the hunt; she evidently learned how to shoot pretty well over the summer! What a girl!*

Midway through about the third day of the hunt I noticed that I had a particularly runny nose, but I felt great and thought that maybe it was just the change in the climate or the change in the vegetation and brush pollen to which I was having a little allergic reaction. But by the next day I could tell that I was indeed coming down with a cold. Small wonder. After about 20 hours of confinement in a packed Airbus 320 with people from all over the earth, it would have been more of a wonder NOT to have come down with some kind of respiratory ailment. And then by the next day, Lorrie too began having symptoms, and by the last several days of the hunt we were both blowing our noses and coughing, and there were wads of damp "white gold" (i.e. toilet tissue) stuffed in our pockets, day pack, and small trash can that we had taken from our room to use in the truck. In spite of having colds, we never missed a beat, and still enjoyed getting up at five o'clock each day to experience this once-in-a-lifetime opportunity. Our attitude was so positive that we were going to have a good time that only a nearby nuclear holocaust could have changed it!

Our fabulous cook, Zelda, came through with excellent dishes at every meal.

Day four started like the others, with a light breakfast and out to the truck by six. By now my cold was in full bloom, but our focus was still on finding and bagging a gemsbok, which to me would be the prize trophy of the entire hunt. We had seen a few—always on a fast move—and had unsuccessfully stalked a few, so maybe today would be the day to add the gemsbok to the "bagged" list. Initially we drove the roads and trails for a couple of hours, and then the PH decided that we should sit in a blind at a waterhole for a while and see what developed. Jean-Louis and Andries stretched a piece of army-drab canvas between two trees, piled up some dead branches and brush to each side, and set three plastic chairs behind the canvas. Andries took the truck about a half-mile down the road to get out of sight, and Lorrie, the PH, and I took our seats behind the blind and began our wait. The rule in the blind is that you stay absolutely quiet, and sit rock-solid still. The animals would pick up movement before they would pick up shape, and if we were downwind from the water hole we might get lucky. We

Wildebeest "back strap" was cooked with coals shoveled from the fire pit. Jean-Louis talking with lodge owner.

were dressed in fairly neutral colored khaki clothes, and we were told to wear our hats low over our faces. It's stone quiet in the area at first because after the site is disturbed by the truck and our activity, the message seems to get around to all the animals to stay away. After about an hour or so, the animals forget about the disturbance and begin to again move around and go for water. They're extremely cautious as they approach the watering hole because it's been genetically ingrained in them that this is where they have been ambushed by lions and

other predators over the eons. They approach one step at a time, stop-look-listen, then approach a few more steps and stop-look-listen, until they reach the water, and even then when they extend their necks to drink they move very slowly and even hesitate just before their nose reaches the water. After the first couple of animals take a drink, the others seem to relax and drink more freely, then they roll in the dirt and chase around, oblivious to our presence and spying eyes.

At this waterhole, the first animals to show were a whole tribe of about 30 banded mongoose that passed about 20 feet from us as they headed to the water. The brush to the sides must have been pretty effective at hiding us. A sow warthog and female impala showed up, as did one gemsbok with a broken horn on one side. One lucky gemsbok. After about three hours of watching the water hole and being entertained by animals that we didn't want to shoot, we gave up and headed to the lodge for lunch, or brunch as they called it. The menu for the day included eland hot dogs and curried chutney noodle salad. Very good!

After the peak of the midday heat we were back on the truck at three o'clock. We saw a baboon cross the road, and later tried to stalk a small group of gemsboks that consisted of several cows and one bull. Jean-Louis took me with him on the stalk and asked Lorrie to stay in the truck, figuring that the fewer people for the animals to spot, the better. But as several times before, the animals eluded us and by the end of the day we hadn't even had the rifle on the sticks. We basked in the fading light of another beautiful sunset as we rode the truck back to the lodge for dinner. As we sauntered around the grounds we noticed that one of the big trees at the lodge was the home for a big blue-headed male lizard and his drab-colored mate, each about a foot long. The female was colored to almost perfectly match the bark on the tree, and was well disguised as long as she didn't move. Lorrie noticed some bushes with tiny, light yellow flowers covered with bees, and a small black and white butterfly. The Southern Hemisphere Spring was

bursting forth. At dinner the owner of the property dined with us. Maybe tomorrow would be a more fruitful day here in the bush of South Africa, for a couple of old, novice hunters. In one conversation with our PH we had asked the age of the average hunting client, and were told that most were between about 45 and 65. He thought that not too many folks over age 70 went on safaris in Africa, but of all his aged 70+ clients, that I was probably about the second-best shape. I took the comment as a compliment, head cold notwithstanding.

Day five found us with great expectations of bagging some of the game we were hunting. We had hunted the first two days with no luck but then bagged two animals on day three. Day four was fruitless, and now we had another day, another opportunity, to make up our statistical standing for bagging our six

Driving the roads along the fence line.

animals on this seven-day adventure. So far, there were only two in the bag for four days of hunting, and with only three days left I, and I'm sure the PH, were both feeling the pressure. We began the morning with the usual scouting of the roads and encountered a herd of gemsbok running across the road one by one, and then seconds later they crossed back across the road again one by one as if something was after them at both ends of their path. It may have been the sound of the truck that spooked them, but who knows. Later we got to stalk a gemsbok but it gave us the slip, and then we stalked a couple of boar warthogs with the same results. Later Jean-Louis took us to an old, cattle feed station where he positioned us at a concrete feed trough ne ar a salt lick and a water trough where he thought the animals would be coming for their mid-morning drink. We waited patiently for about an hour and a half before we saw a nice boar warthog approach. As Jean-Louis was assessing him through his binoculars the warthog climbed up on the edge of the trough to drink and gave itself a full side view. It was a good one, and Jean-Louis said to go ahead and shoot it. Like I've said before, the African animals are spooky around the water holes, and hardly

Martin sitting at the watering holes. The concrete feed trough needed seat cushions!

ever stand perfectly still for very long. The warthog walked around a bit as I positioned myself on the shooting sticks, and when it finally showed itself broadside to me I fired. The boar was walking broadside to me from my right to my left when I fired, and I saw the bullet impact in the very middle of its body. My new rifle scope has a variable setting from 2.5- to 10- power magnification, and because we were sitting on a stakeout I had the power up to one of the higher settings, so I'm sure I saw where I hit the animal. But the warthogs are tough and I was stunned when it didn't fall. The big wildebeest must have weighed more than five or six times that of the warthog and it fell like a ton of bricks. But this hog blasted off on a run like he hadn't been touched, heading to my left straight past the water hole for about 50 feet and then away from us into the bush.

We walked where we thought it ran but couldn't find it so Jean-Louis called Andries to bring the truck and let the dogs do some tracking. The dogs were pretty well conditioned to the report from the rifle, because as soon as the truck arrived the dogs shot from the bed of the truck and began running around trying to find a blood trail. The PH and I began walking through the brush looking for blood signs, but I didn't think that we were on the right path. Pretty soon we heard the dogs barking and Jean-Louis headed back towards where he thought they were. When we arrived we saw Andries walking slowly, looking down carefully and moving tiny stalks of dry grass with a stick that he was carrying. He was following a blood trail on the grass, but as I watched him track I could see absolutely nothing that gave me a clue that the hog had passed this way, so I asked him to show me what he was looking at. He moved a thin piece of stalk grass, like the stem of a wheat stalk but slimmer, and showed me a tiny spot of blood about the size of the end of a pencil lead. His tracking skills were amazing, but look as we did, we didn't find the wounded warthog. Pretty soon the dogs came back, and we concluded that when the dogs were barking they had probably encountered the warthog, but the warthog outran them. We were told that the warthog's reactions are to either stand and fight, back into a hole, or run away. The Jack Russell terriers, Taz and Vuvu, were short legged, the male was old and the female overweight, and both were much too small to provide a cornering fight with a big boar warthog, so the most plausible conclusion was that it outran them and got away, leaving only a tiny trace of blood that was nearly impossible to follow. Regretfully, I lost my big boar. I really wanted a good specimen of a boar warthog simply for the variety that it would provide on a wall of beautiful plains game, but my shot was off by a mile from the critical area that Lorrie and I had trained all summer to shoot. I don't have any valid excuses for not aiming at the vital heart-lung area right above the top of the front leg. I must have been excited to get to shoot the warthog, and after dropping the big wildebeest, my expectation was that any animal as small as a warthog would drop instantly if hit nearly anywhere with the 180 grain bullet from the .308. I was definitely wrong, and as 'they' say, everything is tougher in Africa. This warthog proved it. We headed back to the lodge for brunch, and ironically were served corn muffins with warthog quiche and warthog sausage. As tasty as it was, it was still hard for me to swallow.

During the afternoon hunt we saw several more warthogs, and I even got another one in my sights, but didn't get the chance for a clean shot. Too much brush, and nothing stood still. We also passed right by a gemsbok standing beneath a tree near the road, probably an old bull or he wouldn't have been alone, but evidently nobody saw it but me. Jean-Louis spotted a couple more gemsbok that we got to stalk, but the closest one finally spooked and they both ran away.

Towards the end of the day we were still searching the roads and trails when Jean-Louis had Andries stop the truck, and Jean-Louis, Lorrie, and I took a walk just before reaching a watering hole. Lorrie was asked to hang back, and Jean-Louis and I continued walking for about a couple hundred yards to the watering hole. We approached the area slowly and quietly and took a position behind some trees and brush about 60 yards away from the watering hole and hunkered down for a wait. It was getting late, and just before sundown a zebra appeared from nowhere, walking out of the brush from our right and heading for the water hole. Shortly behind it following in a straight line was another zebra, and another, then another, and then right in the middle of the group was a beautiful, lone gemsbok, followed by a couple more zebras. By the time the PH assessed the gemsbok with his

Five zebras, well disguised by nature.

binoculars to verify that it was a good specimen that I should shoot, the herd was comfortable with being at the water hole and was mixing it up and rolling in the dirt. By now I was positioned on the sticks and was waiting for a clear shot. First there was a zebra in front of the gemsbok so I couldn't shoot, then one behind the gemsbok so I still couldn't shoot, and now the gemsbok was behind the concrete water container. Finally the gemsbok moved clear from the concrete barrier and other zebras, and was standing broadside right behind a zebra, with both animals looking to the left. I had had the gemsbok in my sights now for what seemed like centuries, and I was getting so amped up that my breathing was heavy and my rifle was swaying with each beat of my pounding heart, the crosshairs of the scope wandering from the nose to the tail of this huge gemsbok. I finally fired my .308, breaking the dead silence of the setting, and the roar of the shot startled the zebras into instant panic, scattering them in every direction. The one zebra standing immediately in front of the gemsbok instantly reared up on its hind legs as far as it could without falling backwards, and the gemsbok turned around and started walking away to the right. All the zebras shot off like rockets, but the gemsbok was only walking, somewhat stiff legged as I recall in memory, but walking not running, and not falling as I had expected. So as it was about to reach cover I shot again at its quartering silhouette, and I believe I hit him but again he didn't flinch or fall and just continued to walk until he quickly disappeared into the brush in the failing light of the approaching sunset.

As I recall the sight picture through the rifle scope, I believe my shot hit the gemsbok about nine or ten inches behind the shoulder and a couple of inches above the body's midline. The shot was well into the body of the gemsbok, but I had committed the common error of the novice, clearly pointed out in the book "The Perfect Shot" written by the professional hunter and veterinarian Kevin Robertson. He says in his book: *"The unique shape of the gemsbok, with its extremely deep neck and chest and prominently high withers, can make the placement of a killing first shot confusing and difficult. There is a tendency with these antelope—as with the similarly shaped wildebeest—to shoot too high up the body in the chest and neck area. Thus, the standing rule for gemsbok is: Never place your shot above the body's horizontal midline."* All summer I had practiced at the gun range, shooting at posters showing the vital organs of these animals. But like the greenhorn novice that I was, even after carefully studying the pictures in Robertson's book and reading over and over all summer the caution about shooting too high, I did just what he said not to do.

We brought the dogs in to help us track for a while, but it was now getting past sunset and it was becoming hard to see. After scattering about for a while to search for the wounded gemsbok, we all gathered back at the truck to head for the lodge for a late dinner. Our plan was to come back tomorrow morning and continue the search. Surely by then the gemsbok would have fallen and could be found.

On the truck ride back, and at the dinner table, Jean-Louis further discussed the issue of whether or not the bullet hit the gemsbok. And he revisited the issue several times, even into the next day. Obviously it didn't fall and had walked away to disappear in the bush. And we found no blood. Jean-Louis recounted several experiences where hunters had placed high shoulder shots and the bullet had ricocheted into another animal killing the second animal instantly. Observing the zebra that lurched into a hind-stand made him think (he said) that perhaps the bullet ricocheted into it after hitting a solid bone in the gemsbok, or perhaps maybe the bullet ricocheted after hitting the concrete water container. But that didn't explain to me why this gemsbok walked away instead of running like a rocket like all the other animals, and like all the other gemsbok we had spooked on stealthy stalks. Or like the ones we observed jetting beneath the fence at full speed without breaking stride. These animals could really move, and yet with all the startling noise of the rifle shot and panic of the other zebras, this one didn't run away, it walked. Yes, it was definitely hit. And hurt. I was sure I had shot it, so I would buy it, all $1,653 worth, collected or not.

I don't know if Jean-Louis was testing my integrity or my confidence, or was trying to give me a way out of paying for an expensive animal that I wouldn't collect, or if he was playing some kind of ego game, or what. All I know, and what I said, is that in spite of what it might cost me (it was his call) I really thought I shot and wounded the animal. I agonized that I had shot it, only to watch it wobble away to inevitably fall somewhere in the bush where its beautiful head and hide would be ripped up by the hungry predators of the night. I wished I had some plausible, valid excuse for losing two animals in a row in one day. But I didn't. Maybe I could say I had a bad cold.

I was absolutely devastated.

At the end of this fifth full day of hunting I went to bed severely humbled and depressed. My ego was badly bruised by the loss of not just one, but two trophy specimens in one day—the boar warthog in the morning and my prize bull gemsbok in the afternoon. Perhaps I had too much confidence in the killing power of the .308 since my wildebeest and Lorrie's impala had both fallen in one shot. But the wildebeest was killed with a lucky neck spine shot, not where I was initially aiming, and Lorrie's impala was a much smaller and lighter animal than either the wildebeest or gemsbok and the .308 was very lethal on it. My mind reviewed the book "The Perfect Shot" where over and over, animal after animal, big or small, the author emphasized the triangular area for a heart-lung shot, placed right at the top of the front leg just high enough to miss the bone and hit the top part of the heart where all the vital blood vessels converge, and where the bullet will be sure to pass through the heart and a good portion of at least one lung, depending on the position of the animal. Placed here, even a few inches off target, the shot would be lethal, and even though most animals shot through the heart and/or lungs will run, they won't run far and there will be an ample blood trail leading to their fallen remains. I was resolved that it wouldn't happen again. Too much time and planning, and too much money and expectation had been invested in this trip, and I was determined to bring home the trophies that I was set on obtaining. The remaining two days would be a pressure test, and statistically I was in the short end of the probability of getting all six of my animals on this seven-day hunt. Five of the seven days were gone and only two animals were in the bag. It crossed my mind that after losing two animals in a row, maybe (but just maybe) the scope had gone out of zero, and needed to be reset. In my heart I knew the rifle and scope were right on, but tomorrow we'd go to the target range first thing before heading out to hunt. I was desperate to have something on which to build some confidence.

Dinner on the evening of day five was a blesbok-and-beans casserole with a top crust of baked cheese, served with yellow rice and a side dish of mixed butternut squash and pumpkin. Dessert was marshmallow-cherry vanilla pudding with ice cream on the side. The entire dinner was delicious and it served as comfort food to sooth my tortured soul. But what I really wanted was a tall, stiff drink.

Typical termite mound. They were all over, and about as hard as concrete.

On the next-to-last, sixth day of hunting, the previous evening's dinner of blesbok must have inspired Jean-Louis to bring up the subject of us hunting the blesbok. Originally Lorrie had intended to shoot an impala and a blesbok, and I had intended to shoot a gemsbok and a warthog. So far, of our original list only the impala had been taken, and after she shot the impala Lorrie felt satisfied that she had accomplished her personal goal of coming to Africa and collecting a really nice trophy animal. She had stalked many blesbok before shooting the impala, but since shooting the impala she didn't have the desire to shoot a blesbok or anything else. The PH picked up on this. Meanwhile, I had been focusing on my prize gemsbok and a warthog, neither of which I seemed destined or lucky enough to get. Early in the hunt, once we got to thinking about the once-in-a-lifetime probability of us ever doing it again, we decided that we'd try to also take a wildebeest and a red hartebeest in addition to the original four animals that we had listed on all the paperwork that contracted us for this hunt. Jean-Louis made his living off of these animals, and only four of the least expensive animals available were barely worth his entire week of work, so on the first day of the hunt he had offered to add to the list of our original four, a wildebeest and red hartebeest at a discounted price. I was happy with the offer and considered it a generous gesture and great opportunity to take a couple more nice trophy animals.

I had shot the wildebeest earlier, and after taking the impala Lorrie hadn't mentioned blesbok in days, and now I was focused on taking the gemsbok, hartebeest, and warthog. So it left the question in the mind of Jean-Louis as to whether or not we still wanted to shoot a blesbok. Was it OFF the list, or just the least priority but still ON the list. He was somewhat irritated at the prospect of the blesbok being off the list since he had committed to the hartebeest and wildebeest at a discounted price, and that I had already taken the wildebeest and now seemed to want to cut the blesbok out of the hunt. We had been seeing blesbok but had not stopped to pursue them, evidently because of this uncertainty and misunderstanding of our goals, in both his mind and ours. I believe in HIS mind, he had offered the wildebeest and hartebeest to us at a discount only on the condition that we would still take all four of the original animals for which we came to hunt, but we were under the impression from our representative, John Campbell, that we could add or subtract any animal we wanted from their price list. After all, this was a fair-chase hunt and there was no guarantee that we would get ANY animal—period, contracted or not.

After discussing the issue and clearing the air, we began to look for blesbok in addition to the gemsbok, warthog, and red hartebeest that we still hadn't harvested. We had taken two animals in five days, and now our expectation was to take the remaining four in only two short days. It seemed impossible, and statistically improbable considering how the hunt had gone so far. It was up to the PH to find the animals and get us a shooting opportunity, but it would ultimately be up to me to complete this hunt successfully. Lorrie was done shooting and was just enjoying the experience as she battled her head cold.

So on day six, as per the established routine, we headed out to hunt at six o'clock, but stopping first at the target range to make sure that the rifle and scope were accurate. From 100 yards the sights were right on as I grouped three shots closely around the zero point of the paper target, which Jean-Louis collected and carefully folded and put into his pocket, presumably as physical proof that yesterday's errant shots were because of the shooter and not the gun. Hmm.

Again it was up and down the roads and trails, looking for the right game, the right sex, the right horns, and the right opportunity and situation to be successful in collecting any of the four remaining animals that we sought. We saw kudu, giraffes, a herd of wildebeest and zebras, a sable, and of course warthogs. We always saw warthogs, but they were hard to get because they just don't stand still for long. It seems that EVERYTHING wants to eat them so in addition to being prolific breeders, they move constantly to help ensure their survival. We were occasionally seeing everything we wanted to hunt except for the red hartebeest. We had seen the two old bulls right near the road on the second day, but since then the hartebeest had been hard to find. Even the motion-sensitive cameras that had been strategically placed around the watering holes had until now failed to record the presence of any hartebeest.

We stopped by the area where I had shot the gemsbok the evening before, and couldn't find any sign of it. Lorrie was mesmerized at following Andries while he tried to pick up a trail of the gemsbok. His slow but steady steps proved to her that humans could walk clear across Africa at this pace because they'd never burn all their energy if they never broke a sweat. After four people and two dogs failed to find the gemsbok in an hour of searching in the 102-degree heat, we decided to call it off and make use of the short amount of time that we still had to collect the remaining four animals that we wanted. I still felt bad about the demise of the beautiful creature, and looked forward to a more rewarding shooting experience if ever again given the chance.

Eventually, we spotted another herd of blesbok as the truck crept along the road. We had stalked them more than any of the other animals that we were pursuing, but their many eyes were a good defense and we hadn't scored any shots. Suddenly Jean-Louis snapped his fingers, Andries stopped the truck, and grabbing his shooting sticks as he bailed off the tailgate the PH whispered those magic words of expectation: "Grab your gun!" We headed into the bush and like usual the herd would move one way, stop, and then move back and stop, and eventually Jean-Louis glassed the blesbok he wanted me to shoot and he set up the sticks in front of me. He spotted a mature bull looking right at me like all the other 20, and made it clear which one he wanted me to shoot. The bull finally turned broadside to us, and from about 70 or 80 yards away, I squeezed off a shot aimed at that vital area that I swore to myself that I would hit if ever given another chance, and the blesbok dropped in his tracks. The PH did his job, I did my job, and the .308 did its job. We walked to the beast and I was so breathless from the adrenalin that I was about to burst. The shot had been "the perfect shot" and this critter was in the bag. Upon seeing the well-placed bullet hole in the blesbok, Jean-Louis looked at me, grinned, and stated that

I had "redeemed myself" but he didn't extend a congratulatory hand or say "good job" as he did when I shot the first animal of the hunt, the wildebeest on the morning of the third day. According to the SCI measurements, my wildebeest and this blesbok would later prove to be two of the nicest trophies that I would harvest. Andries and the PH loaded it onto a canvas and proceeded to drag it to the truck where we posed it, with me grinning ear to ear as I sat behind it just far enough away from the camera to make the blesbok look as big as possible but with me still in focus. We headed for the skinning shed and since it was about time for brunch, we left Andries to do his work while we went to the lodge to eat brunch. Three down, three to go, and only one and a half more days to hunt.

The way to photograph the trophy—close to the camera, with hunter far in the background. This blesbok scored in the Silver category in the SCI records. And to think we almost stopped hunting for a blesbok!

By now Lorrie and I both had full-blown (pun intended) colds and the white gold was being used extensively. We had appropriately used the time of the peak heat of the day between brunch and three o'clock for naps, and that hour or so of daytime rest kept our energy up for the remaining hours of the daily hunts.

At three o'clock we were back on the truck. Jean-Louis began focusing on finding where the red hartebeest had been hanging out, but was having a hard time finding them. He had placed a motion activated camera at a watering hole, and when we checked it this morning it showed that on the two previous mornings, two red hartebeest bulls had come to the water early, at 5:30 one morning, and at 5:31 the next. He decided that if we didn't get one today, that tomorrow we'd try to get up real early and post ourselves at that water hole before 5:30 and get ourselves a hartebeest. In the meantime we still had to get the gemsbok and warthog that were still on the list. After hunting the roads for a while, Jean-Louis decided to stake out a watering hole for the remaining hours of the day so we all went back to the blind where we had seen the boar warthog that I had shot and lost. After a while we were seeing

After freshening up for lunch, Lorrie sat in the sun to dry her hair.

28

several species of game, but no hartebeest and no warthogs, and then surprisingly a big gemsbok came sauntering up to the watering hole so I quickly got positioned on the shooting sticks. It turned out to be

an old cow, but Jean-Louis glassed it carefully, and judging by its great set of horns and the absence of an extended belly, he decided it wasn't pregnant and would be a good specimen to shoot. It was evidently out of the breeding pool (because at this time of Spring it would otherwise be pregnant) and it would be okay to shoot, and besides, the gemsbok cows were one of the few African game animals whose horns were judged just the same as the bulls. And this one had a beautiful set of long horns worthy of any trophy wall. Although the female gemsbok can have longer horns than some bulls, their horns are usually more slender, and sometimes they are curved, bent, or not symmetrical. But this cow was a very good trophy specimen. Needless to say my nerves were in jangles. The previous experience of losing the bull gemsbok was still fresh in my mind, and my confidence was still delicate in spite of

bagging the blesbok with a perfect shot. Now all I had to do was a repeat performance of the blesbok. Being patient and careful paid off, because as soon as the cow turned broadside to me Jean-Louis's "three second" warning sounded in my brain, and I drew down on the Perfect Shot triangle and pulled the trigger.

Again the rifle roared, the animals scattered, and instantly the gemsbok kicked into high gear and headed from right to left away from the watering area, and then ran, not walked, away from us into the brush. Fear gripped my soul as all I could see was more disappointment at the thought of losing another prize gemsbok. But one look at Andries said it all as I asked

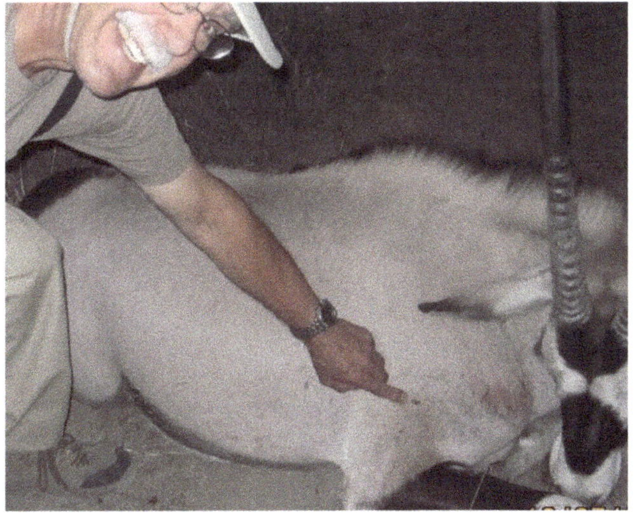

him for confirmation of my hit, because he grinned widely and said "lots of blood squirting." Even in the magnified image of my scope I didn't see any blood, so I

quickly walked immediately to where I saw the cow disappear into the bush and walked only a short distance and there she was, dead and hunkered down on all four legs like some cattle do when they are resting in a field. I went back to the spot where she had been when I fired, but I didn't see the blood on the ground until Andries pointed it out to me. It was plainly there in the dry, loose dirt, but I didn't know what to look for until Andries showed me. After getting educated about what blood looks like in the dirt, I saw that there was plenty of it. Upon closer examination of the cow gemsbok, I again could see the results of the bullet hitting the area just above the top of the front leg. Death to the animal was sure and sudden. My confidence was building, but again I

29

don't recall Jean-Louis extending his hand in congratulations and saying "well done" even though I do recall the joy that Lorrie showed at my success. By now it was nearly past sunset and the light was fading fast. We positioned the cow and took some photos, and afterwards drove the truck over to the downed animal so that we could use the winch to hoist the large antelope into the back of the truck. Gemsbok can weigh about 550 pounds, way too much to be tossed around, so the winch came in handy to load it without damaging its hide or horns. We headed back to the skinning shed and lodge again, for Andries to do his work and for us to get a late dinner. It was a fruitful day. By bagging the blesbok in the morning and the gemsbok in the evening the odds for a final successful hunt were improving, but we still had two more animals to harvest in just one remaining day. It would be a challenge, but I appreciated that this really was a fair chase hunt.

Finally, the payoff for a shot well placed on a nice trophy gemsbok.

Part III – The Follow-up and Conclusion

Def: *redeem (to redeem oneself)—to do something that compensates for poor past performance or behavior*

Earlier in conversation Jean-Louis had made a statement about the ways and superstitions of the bush. He said that the bush gives you what you deserve. In thinking back, I find it interesting that on this hunt everything seemed to happen in twos. The first two days were fruitless. The next day we got two of our animals. Then two more days passed without getting anything, and on day five I shot two animals but lost those two animals. Now on day six we again harvested two animals in one day. Whatever the superstitions, the statistics were definitely improving, but it was still a big guess as to whether or not we'd get two more animals in one day, back to back. It was unfortunate that it was so late by the time we got back, cleaned up, and had dinner, because I would have liked to have savored the memories of the day over a glass of scotch, or sat around the fire pit and talked. But it was now late, and we were told to be up early so that we could be on the truck by five o'clock in order to stake out the water hole where the two bull hartebeest had been coming at 5:30. We still had colds, so we headed to bed to get our much needed rest. At least sleep would come easy after such a successful day. Both of the 'boks' were in the bag, finally, and my confidence was being restored. We were pretty happy with ourselves and looked forward to more fun for just one more day of activity "outside the box."

The sun rising behind Lorrie's nose as she sits rock-solid still in the blind. She did the great camo job on her hat with black and brown shoe polish before we left home.

Day seven, the last official day of the hunt, came early. It was still dark when we arose, and only a quick bite for breakfast was all we wanted if we were to get to the blind before the hartebeest came through.

We were full of hope on this last day of the hunt and the sun was just rising as we were driving out to the blind. On the way we passed a herd of the large eland, and when Jean-Louis spotted the remains of a waterbuck lying near the road he stopped to evaluate it.

Since today would be the last day of the hunt our PH Jean-Louis needed to stay at the lodge to do some paperwork, so he left us with Andries at the blind overlooking the waterhole where the two old bull hartebeest had been

Eland, growing up to 1500 pounds, are the world's largest antelope and are considered by many to be the best eating.

coming at 5:30. We situated ourselves in our chairs, sat back to relax, and began the wait. As day broke, it seemed that all kinds of animals came to the water hole except the hartebeest. We watched a herd of impala come in, and then another herd of impala came in and the competing rams chased each other around in their show of dominance until they were passing right by our blind. Evidently we were holding dead still and were adequately disguised and hidden by the brush piled up at our sides. Later a jackal came to the concrete water vessel, jumped up on it and walked around its perimeter. I viewed the jackal in my scope and was amazed at how healthy and beautiful it was. It looked somewhat like a red fox, with a bushy tail, but larger and with longer legs. I loved sitting at the blinds because you never knew what you'd get to see. Eventually the ubiquitous warthog showed up. We fully expected it, but it was a sow with two large pigs. The offspring looked pretty big, and since this was the last day to fill our bag, Andries called Jean-Louis on the two-way radio to discuss the idea of taking a sow warthog. At this late date in the hunt there was no guarantee that we'd get another chance to shoot a

Predators don't leave much. Our PH estimated that this waterbuck had been dead for about two months.

warthog, either boar or sow, and since the offspring were so grown, the PH gave Andries the go ahead. I hesitated for a moment due to the language barrier between us, as I wanted it to be perfectly clear to all parties that I was reluctant to shoot a sow unless I was perfectly sure that it was okay. Andries assured me that it was okay with Jean-Louis. The sticks and the rifle were all set and I was peering through the scope when the sow got to the position of hoisting itself to the brim of the trough for a drink. When she finished drinking and set her front feet on the ground I carefully aimed for my "perfect shot" above the shoulder and fired. Like all the other animals shot this way, she

My view in the blind of the concrete water trough.

took off in a full-speed run, from my right to the left, and disappeared into the brush. I quickly ran to the point where she was when I fired, and this time I didn't need any help finding the blood trail. It looked like someone had spilled a bucket of red paint while they were running and the trail was so obvious that a

blind person could have followed it. With that much damage and blood loss it just couldn't have gone very far. Andries called Jean-Louis to bring the truck and the dogs, and when he arrived the dogs immediately found the blood and took off on the scent. We all walked right to the warthog as we followed the copious trail of blood. About halfway to the pig we found a chunk of tissue about an inch or more wide and a couple of inches long that turned out to be a piece of lung tissue. Very shortly we found the pig, stone cold dead with large blood soaks on both sides of its body. Upon turning the pig over to the side of the exit wound, you could see major blood vessels from the heart hanging out of the skin. The damage that the 180-grain .308 Barnes bullet did was amazing, and the fact that this pig ran the distance that it ran is good testimony as to how tough these animals really are. After seeing the physical damage it amazed me that the hog even took one step, yet it ran probably 60 or more yards before it dropped. Interestingly, the entry hole of the bullet on all the other animals was just the size of the bullet, cleanly poking a hole in the hide and showing little exterior damage. But with this warthog, the entry hole looked as big as a broomstick and lots of tissue damage was clearly visible! Why the bullet did so much external damage upon entry must have been due to it expanding before it even penetrated the skin—the skin of the warthog being that tough! This graphic description is furnished only to emphasize the saying that "everything's tougher in Africa." My oh my, I should say so.

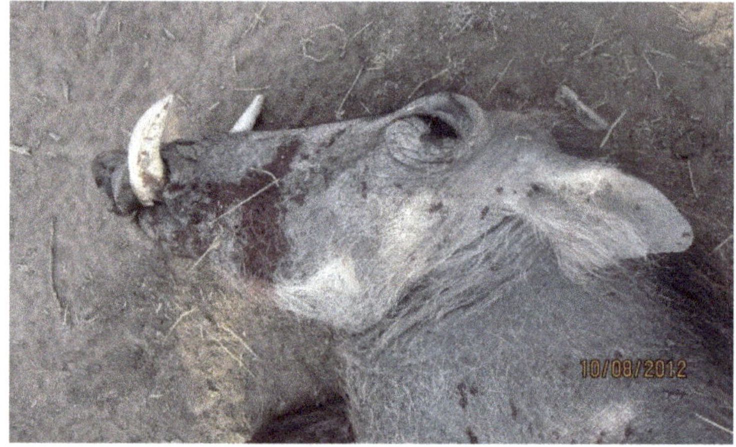

Super tough, and with looks that only a mother could love!

Lorrie and I took some photos of the slain sow warthog, but since it wasn't trophy size or a big boar with impressive tusks nobody else bothered. To me and Lorrie she's beautiful, and she'll grace our wall right along with the other game trophies. The PH and Andries carried the warthog to the truck and we headed back to the skinning shed.

We now had five of the six game animals we wanted. It was a good morning at the watering hole stake out, but the hartebeest were still avoiding us. Evidently they came a little earlier than usual and we missed them, or the word got around that we'd be waiting for them. The sow warthog didn't get the memo. When we started hunting earlier in the week the moon had been totally full, and the PH said that the full moon was a significant influence on hunting, because with enough light the animals would feed and water by night so that they wouldn't have to roam around in the heat of the day. The temperature had been 104 degrees one day, and 108 on another, so it was likely that the animals were taking advantage of the light, although the full moon was now on the wane on this last full day of the hunt.

The sun was getting low, time was running out, and the hartebeest were elusive.

After brunch we were back on the truck at two o'clock instead of three, and we continued driving around searching for a hartebeest. It was the last animal on our list and we saw several and even stalked them, but they saw us too. End of story. While driving we came across a beautiful cat, somewhat like a small American cougar, but with pointy nose and ears like a domestic cat, and a long graceful tail. Upon surprising it as it sat on its kill of a 2-foot lizard, it stared at us for a moment then bolted into the bush. Jean-Louis retrieved the lizard for us so we could get a closer look and take pictures. We continued our hunt in some

areas not usually visited by us during the past week, and by the time the sun began to set, I reconciled to myself that it had been a fabulous hunt even if we didn't get the red hartebeest. It finally got dark enough that I commented to Jean-Louis that I wouldn't be able to see anything through my rifle scope even if we spotted a hartebeest, and that the hunt must be officially over. Upon which comment, he retorted that it must be time to resort to all the tools at our disposal, and he dug out a huge spotlight from the compartment beneath the seats below me and Lorrie.

Last sunset of the hunt. We'll miss this!

Now the hunt was taking on a new and different feel, as we drove through the night seeing the bright eyes of animals reflected in the spotlight. On this last day of the hunt the sky started showing some high, thin overcast, hinting that the dry winter was about to come to an end, but the evening sky was now crystal clear and the unfamiliar stars of the Southern Hemisphere sparkled overhead. We drove down by the Crocodile River and saw monkeys, the bright, big, red eyes of exotic birds, and the eyes of other animals

Even Lorrie's shoes glistened in the bright light as she documented the bagging of the red hartebeest.

that we probably didn't want to know about. Jean-Louis made the comment that the hunt would be over when HE said it was over, so we didn't argue and just sat back to enjoy the experience. The plains game animals would bed down in the grass once it got dark, and if by chance we spotted a hartebeest it might still be possible to add it to our list of bagged trophies. Remember as previously stated, this was private property, with no game laws governing these common animals. Maybe it was different with endangered species or in some other circumstances or conditions, but not here and not with red hartebeest, so the spotlight was just another tool at our disposal. We continued to hunt well into the darkness long after sunset.

It must have been between seven and eight o'clock when we finally spotted a hartebeest bedded down for the night not too far from the road. Jean-Louis quickly glassed it with his binoculars and determined that it was an old bull, appropriate for shooting if only it would stand up and show itself. I eagerly got my rifle ready as he continued to hold the light on the hartebeest. I was ready to shoot if it stood up, but then it got up and immediately turned away from us and began to move off into the bush. Quickly Jean-Louis said to shoot it at the base of the tail, and I remembered the stories in "The Perfect Shot" about taking a 'Texas heart shot' right up the anus of a departing animal, a shot which has a good chance of either breaking the lower spine or shattering the hips or pelvis, which will drop the animal instantly. I didn't have any time to assess the situation, or consider the consequences of missing or losing another wounded animal, so I used my best judgment, centered the crosshairs of the scope just below the base of the tail, and fired. The back half of the stricken animal fell instantly, and the front half followed. I ran through the dry, knee-deep grass to get closer to finish off the wounded animal, but the dogs beat me to it and were in the way. They were as excited as I was and were running all around the mortally wounded hartebeest. I surely didn't want to shoot and injure one of the dogs as that would be unforgivable. The PH called his dogs away and when they got clear, I shot the hartebeest through the lower neck near the body, hoping to kill it instantly with a spine shot. The animal moaned and expired, and I finally filled my bag, although the final shot blew some of the hair off of the hide since I was so close when I fired. It'll be interesting to see what the taxidermist does to the wall mounting to disguise the bare spot. This red hartebeest was old and skinny, and Jean-Louis commented that even though they had been putting out feed at some of the watering holes, some of the old, weak animals weren't feeding, and he thought that this might be one of them. It was humane that we took the hartebeest rather than leave it to the impending ravage by predators.

Even though it was getting pitch dark, with the aid of the big spotlight we managed to position the red hartebeest for a good photo session before loading it into the back of the truck. It was late by the time we reached the lodge, but the faithful cook had a wonderful hot dinner waiting for us. After dinner, and without a lot of ceremony, we went to our room to pack so that we could have a smooth and quick departure from the lodge in the morning. By the time we would complete some paperwork and payments at the main office in Thabazimbi, and perhaps shop at the bazaar or market, it would take all day to get to the airport. Now the hunt was really officially over and we could sleep peacefully knowing that we had accomplished our goal.

Elephant skull at Numzaan Safaris' main office in Thabazimbi. South Africa.

We awoke on that last morning proud of ourselves that the hunt had been completely successful, and that we old folks had actually bagged all the animals that we contracted for on this real, honest-to-goodness South African hunting safari. After breakfast, I took a ride to the skinning shed with Jean-Louis to watch the owner of the Swift Dip Company do the accessioning of the heads, hides, and horns of all the animals that we collected. The PH even included the skull and tusks of a boar warthog that Andries found while driving around in the bush. Swift Dip will do the initial processing of the heads, hides, and horns and crate them for shipping to Seattle in about January or February. The process takes at least three months. The warthog boar skull and tusks will be nice to have for a comparison to the dainty sow that we hope to eventually display.

The date was October 9th. We had noticed that the sky was changing and that it had been unusually windy the past couple of days, and today it was obvious that the rainy season was on its way. The sky was overcast and there were reports of rain in Johannesburg. We were the last hunting clients for the season, and now the rains would set in; we had timed our hunt almost perfectly. If however I was to do it again, I'd schedule the hunt for about the second or third week of September instead of the first week of October. I believe the weather would still be nice and dry, but the temperature might be a bit cooler.

Photos don't do justice to the beauty of the jacaranda trees gracing the town streets.

We said our goodbyes (and gave our tips) to the staff at the lodge, and headed to the Numzaan Safaris main office in Thabazimbi. There we settled our bill with the bookkeeper, and made sure that all of our paperwork and payments were in place for the preparation and eventual shipping of all the trophy heads, hides, and horns. Andries rode with us to Thabazimbi and we towed a small trailer that contained our luggage and gun and a lot of Jean-Louis' personal supplies and equipment. We tipped Andries as he left us at Thabazimbi. The roads in the area are narrow and far from being safe, and Jean-Louis drove pretty fast, but we just tightened our seatbelts, and hoped that all would go well. We got a call on the truck radio that we'd have to delay for a few minutes while another employee caught up with us to get a briefcase that was accidentally left in our truck. I was adamant that we get to the airport a full three hours prior to the plane departure, as per the instructions from the South African Airlines, but Jean-Louis was determined to get us there on his schedule, which seemed to be about a half-hour later than what I wanted. He was also determined that we would stop at the market for a quick shopping spree, which obviously would cut more into our time. He was going by the time for transit to the final destination as calculated by his GPS, but the GPS had no awareness of the detours he wanted to take to his house, the stop for the errant briefcase, the side trip to pick up his little girl from school, and any traffic problems that might arise. And the GPS also couldn't predict any delays from the social unrest that was occurring due to the transportation strike that had been in progress all the time we had been in South Africa. But he didn't seem to care; he was in control at the wheel of the truck and he let us know it, until he seemed to soften his stance when I quietly asked Lorrie if we could still stop any payments made to the Visa credit card.

Flowering tree at the home of PH Jean-Louis Viljoen.

Native trees along the driveway to the home of our PH Jean-Louis, Thabazimbi, South Africa.

We took a few photos through the windows of the truck as we drove, and we're glad we stopped for a few souvenirs at the bazaar, however brief it might have been, as we plan to place them on the wall amongst the game trophies. We got to the airport in time to check in, clear the gun with the customs and the South African Police Service, and make it to our flight. Jean-Louis dropped us off out front and went to park the truck and then later met us at the SAPS office where we temporarily forgot where we put a vital piece of paper to document our rifle. After a couple of anxious moments we found it and everything was fine. Jean-Louis had delivered us in good shape to the airport, so we said our goodbyes to him and he left. From there it was smooth sailing through the airport with the aid of a couple of attendants, and before we knew it we were on the Airbus 320 headed to home by the same route as we had come. Without our knowledge, the connecting plane departure at Dulles was delayed by a couple of hours, so the frantic transition that we expected when we first landed never happened. We were nearly running from one concourse to another to make our change since Dulles was our first stop in the USA and we had to claim all our luggage and gun and then recheck-in through customs and airport security. Our paperwork showed that we had about an hour to change flights, but the flight schedule had changed during the week we were hunting, and it turned out that we had about three hours, which was plenty of time for the plane change and a meal to boot.

Upon arrival at Seattle everything went smoothly also, including catching the shuttle bus, and before we knew it we were being met at the Bellingham Airport by our faithful friend Jennifer Corbell who took us to our house in Blaine. We continued to take the malaria pills for another week after we arrived home, and the cold we imported hung around forever, manifesting itself as a slight, tickling cough deep in the chest.

About two weeks after getting back home we received an e-mail message from Isabelle, the finance and scheduling person with Numzaan Safaris, that our wounded bull gemsbok had been found dead and

Nice house in Thabazimbi.

The rural roads weren't too good and driving on the left made me uncomfortable, but we were in good hands.

Professional Hunter Jean-Louis Viljoen

that the PH Jean-Louis would salvage the skull for us and measure the horns for the SCI scoring. There was still time to send the skull and horns to the Swift Dip Company and have them added to our other

After about 30 hours of travel, we were glad to see Jennifer Corbell at the Bellingham airport.

trophies, and have them shipped all together. The price for the animal and the cost for the extra processing and shipping of the skull and horns will have to be paid, but it will be comforting to me personally that some part of that beautiful trophy animal will be salvaged. At least we'll now have the proof of shooting the first bull gemsbok, and have the bull's horns to compare with those of the cow.

When completed, the trophy wall at home will be a great item for conversation, but the conclusion to this adventure won't be over until we actually have the trophies on the wall of our living room—complete with souvenirs—which is anticipated to be about July of 2013. Let's hope that the hides, heads, and horns have all been properly handled and treated, and that the taxidermy studio (Buzzi and Sandy Cook of Olympic Taxidermy Studio, Inc., in North Bend, Washington) does a good job mounting them for display.

Summation

The extensive safari or a simple hunt is more, much more, than just the shooting of an animal. The actual act of shooting takes only seconds—brace, aim, fire—but the planning and preparations, both physical and mental, are what makes for the excitement and the memories. The entire scope of the hunting experience is what matters, not just that you get to shoot an animal. The shooting of the animal is, however, the culmination of all the planning, expense, effort, training, and skill, and if the end result is that you collect a trophy it is an experience not to be forgotten. But if you shoot an animal and don't collect it, that also is an experience not to be forgotten, because the disappointment, frustration, and feelings that you experience after a missed or poorly placed shot are forever burned into your memory. On this trip I clearly recall the vision of the successful shooting and collecting of six animals, but I remember much more vividly the emotional impact and scrambled feelings of not collecting the two animals that I mortally wounded that got away. We could bring home the processed heads, hides, and horns from the hunt, but the meat from the animals had to remain in South Africa, where it is distributed for the locals or to commercial outlets.

Much of how you feel about hunting is a matter of your personal ethics. As pointed out in the introduction there is a big difference in hunters. Some, like Teddy Roosevelt, shot as many animals as they could shoot, with many shots taken at great distances that would have a high probability of only wounding the animal and eventually losing it. To them, the fun and pleasure was in the actual shooting, and they had little regard for the final disposition of the animal. But to others, the chase, challenge, drama, expectation, and uncertainty of the outcome, was more valuable, and it also considered the element of a man's character. The pleasure for those hunters was much broader, and their interpretation of "sport" considered a man's character and ethics and included great respect for the game animals.

"Often a man's character is unknown until it is challenged" …….

One last thought……   In our modern day there are those that wrinkle their nose at the very idea of killing an animal, but I would submit that there is hardly a human on the entire planet that hasn't eaten some amount of meat at some time in their life. Those repulsed at the killing of an animal are oblivious to the reality of where our food comes from. It is simply a matter of them not understanding the true nature of man and the fact that he has, from his primal ancestral beginnings, always been a hunter and a meat eater. His very survival, and our very existence, is because man hunted. The history of hunting has been well documented and honorably celebrated for thousands of years by Pharaohs, Kings, and Presidents. Ethically hunting animals is an honorable profession, an honorable sport, and a character building experience available to anyone that pursues it with the right attitude and frame of mind.

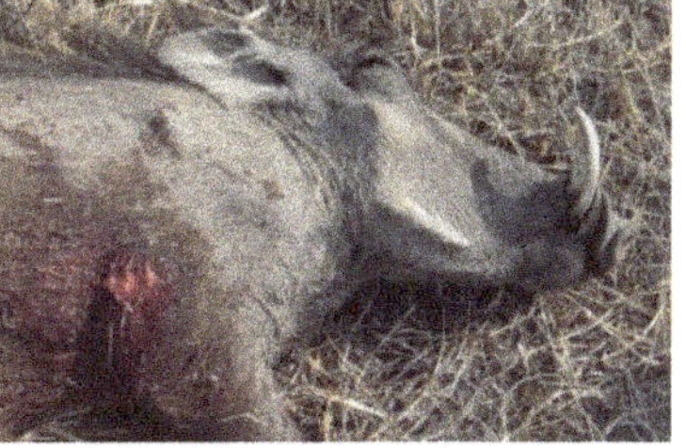